MW01124265

Sorting Out Mammals

Everything You Want to Know About Marsupials, Carnivores, Herbivores, and More!

Samuel G. Woods

BLACKBIRCH PRESS, INC.

WOODBRIDGE, CONNECTICUT

Published by Blackbirch Press, Inc.
260 Amity Road
Woodbridge, CT 06525
e-mail: staff@blackbirch.com
Web site: www.blackbirch.com

Printed in Hong Kong

10 9 8 7 6 5 4 3 2 1

Photo Credits
Cover: ©Corel Corporation; pages 4-10, 11 (top and middle), 12, 14, 16-18, 19 (top and middle), 20, 21, 23, 24 (top), 25, 26, 27 (top and bottom), 29, 30: ©Corel Corporation; pages 11 (bottom), 15, 19 (bottom), 22, 24 (bottom), 27 (middle left), 28, 31: ©PhotoDisc; page 13: ©Peter Ward/Bruce Coleman/PNI.

Library of Congress Cataloging-in-Publication Data
Woods, Samuel G.
Sorting out mammals: everything you want to know about marsupials, carnivores, herbivores, and
more! / Samuel G. Woods.—1st ed.
        p.   cm. — (Sorting out)
    Includes bibliographical references.
    Summary: Describes the characteristics and behavior of different categories of mammals, including
hoofed mammals, carnivores, insectivores, egg-laying mammals, primates, and more.
    ISBN 1-56711-372-9
    1. Mammals Juvenile literature. [1. Mammals.] I. Title. II. Title: Mammals. III. Series.
QL706.2.W66 1999
599—dc21   99-14600
                                                                                                  CIP
                                                                                                  AC

Contents

Even-Toed Hoofed Mammals

Scientific Name: *Order Artiodactyla*
How to Say It: AR·TEE·O·DAK·TIE·LUH

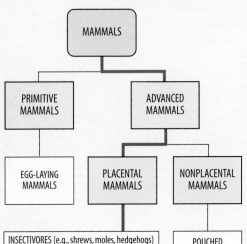

MAMMALS
- PRIMITIVE MAMMALS
  - EGG-LAYING MAMMALS
- ADVANCED MAMMALS
  - PLACENTAL MAMMALS
  - NONPLACENTAL MAMMALS
    - POUCHED MAMMALS (e.g., kangaroos, koalas, oppossums)

PLACENTAL MAMMALS:

INSECTIVORES (e.g., shrews, moles, hedgehogs)

BATS

FLYING LEMURS

TOOTHLESS MAMMALS (e.g., anteaters, sloths, armadillos)

PANGOLINS

PRIMATES (e.g., lemurs, tarsiers, monkeys, apes, humans)

RODENTS (e.g., squirrels, rats, beavers, mice, porcupines)

RABBITS, HARES, PIKAS

WHALES, DOLPHINS, PORPOISES

CARNIVORES (e.g., cats, dogs, weasels, bears, hyenas)

SEALS, SEA LIONS, WALRUSES

AARDVARKS

HYRAXES AND DASSIES

ELEPHANTS

SEA COWS (e.g., manatees, dugongs)

ODD-TOED HOOFED MAMMALS (e.g., horses, rhinoceroses, tapirs)

EVEN-TOED MAMMALS (e.g., hogs, cattle, camels, hippopotamuses)

Giraffe

4

Hippopotamus

Llama

Camel

NOTEPAD

These mammals are further broken down into two main groups. One group has four-chambered stomachs and chews their cud. The other group doesn't.

Examples of cud-chewers: giraffes, deer, moose, reindeer, elk, pronghorn antelope, cattle, bison, yaks, water buffalo, wildebeests, gazelles, sheep, and goats.

Examples of non-cud-chewers: pigs, peccaries, hippopotamuses, camels, and llamas.

Odd-Toed Hoofed Mammals

Scientific Name: *Order Perissodactyla*
How to Say It: PER•ISS•O•DAK•TIE•LUH

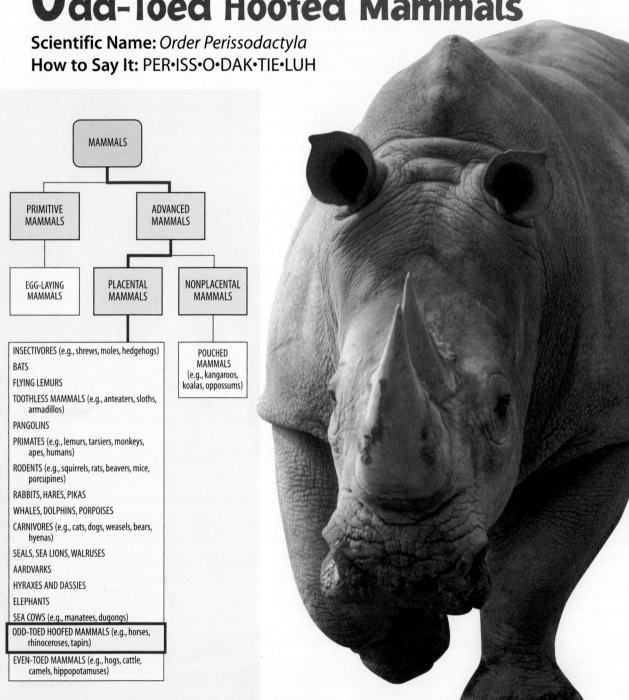

MAMMALS

- **PRIMITIVE MAMMALS**
- **ADVANCED MAMMALS**

- **EGG-LAYING MAMMALS**
- **PLACENTAL MAMMALS**
- **NONPLACENTAL MAMMALS**

INSECTIVORES (e.g., shrews, moles, hedgehogs)

BATS

FLYING LEMURS

TOOTHLESS MAMMALS (e.g., anteaters, sloths, armadillos)

PANGOLINS

PRIMATES (e.g., lemurs, tarsiers, monkeys, apes, humans)

RODENTS (e.g., squirrels, rats, beavers, mice, porcupines)

RABBITS, HARES, PIKAS

WHALES, DOLPHINS, PORPOISES

CARNIVORES (e.g., cats, dogs, weasels, bears, hyenas)

SEALS, SEA LIONS, WALRUSES

AARDVARKS

HYRAXES AND DASSIES

ELEPHANTS

SEA COWS (e.g., manatees, dugongs)

ODD-TOED HOOFED MAMMALS (e.g., horses, rhinoceroses, tapirs)

EVEN-TOED MAMMALS (e.g., hogs, cattle, camels, hippopotamuses)

POUCHED MAMMALS (e.g., kangaroos, koalas, oppossums)

Rhinoceros

Tapir

Zebra

Horses

NOTEPAD

This group of grass-and-plant-eaters includes mammals that have hoofs with an odd number of toes—either 1 or 3 toes. These creatures are broken down into families of the horse-like animals (horses, donkeys, zebras), the tapirs, and the rhinoceroses.

These mammals stand by putting most of their weight on their central toes. The third toe is usually the longest and is the only functional toe that can actually move.

Meat-Eating Mammals (Carnivores)

Scientific Name: *Order Carnivora*
How to Say It: CAR•NEH•VORE•AH

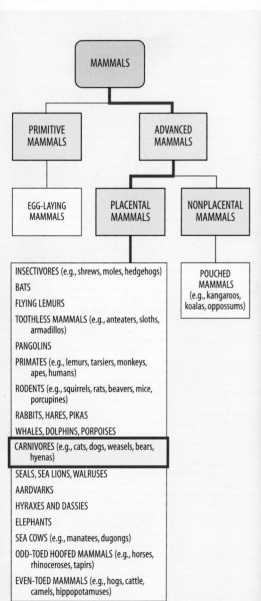

```
                        ┌──────────┐
                        │ MAMMALS  │
                        └──────────┘
              ┌──────────────┴──────────────┐
        ┌──────────┐                  ┌──────────┐
        │PRIMITIVE │                  │ ADVANCED │
        │ MAMMALS  │                  │ MAMMALS  │
        └──────────┘                  └──────────┘
              │                  ┌──────────┴──────────┐
        ┌──────────┐       ┌──────────┐       ┌──────────────┐
        │EGG-LAYING│       │PLACENTAL │       │ NONPLACENTAL │
        │ MAMMALS  │       │ MAMMALS  │       │   MAMMALS    │
        └──────────┘       └──────────┘       └──────────────┘
```

INSECTIVORES (e.g., shrews, moles, hedgehogs)

BATS

FLYING LEMURS

TOOTHLESS MAMMALS (e.g., anteaters, sloths, armadillos)

PANGOLINS

PRIMATES (e.g., lemurs, tarsiers, monkeys, apes, humans)

RODENTS (e.g., squirrels, rats, beavers, mice, porcupines)

RABBITS, HARES, PIKAS

WHALES, DOLPHINS, PORPOISES

CARNIVORES (e.g., cats, dogs, weasels, bears, hyenas)

SEALS, SEA LIONS, WALRUSES

AARDVARKS

HYRAXES AND DASSIES

ELEPHANTS

SEA COWS (e.g., manatees, dugongs)

ODD-TOED HOOFED MAMMALS (e.g., horses, rhinoceroses, tapirs)

EVEN-TOED MAMMALS (e.g., hogs, cattle, camels, hippopotamuses)

POUCHED MAMMALS (e.g., kangaroos, koalas, oppossums)

Lion

Skunk

Polar bear

Fox

Raccoon

NOTEPAD

Scientists organize these animals into two smaller groups. One group has claws that can move in and out of their toes. The other group—also known for having long snouts—has claws that can't move at all.

Examples of mammals with claws that move: cats, lions, tigers, cheetahs, leopards, lynx, bobcats, hyenas, mongooses, and civets.

Examples of mammals with claws that don't move: dogs, wolves, jackals, foxes, bears, raccoons, coatis, martens, weasels, skunks, and otters.

Whales, Dolphins, and Porpoises

Scientific Name: *Order Cetacea*
How to Say It: SEH•TAY•SHAH

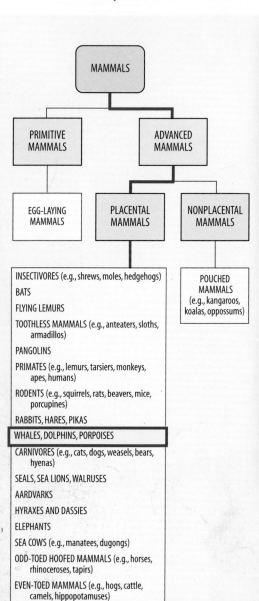

- MAMMALS
  - PRIMITIVE MAMMALS
    - EGG-LAYING MAMMALS
  - ADVANCED MAMMALS
    - PLACENTAL MAMMALS
      - INSECTIVORES (e.g., shrews, moles, hedgehogs)
      - BATS
      - FLYING LEMURS
      - TOOTHLESS MAMMALS (e.g., anteaters, sloths, armadillos)
      - PANGOLINS
      - PRIMATES (e.g., lemurs, tarsiers, monkeys, apes, humans)
      - RODENTS (e.g., squirrels, rats, beavers, mice, porcupines)
      - RABBITS, HARES, PIKAS
      - WHALES, DOLPHINS, PORPOISES
      - CARNIVORES (e.g., cats, dogs, weasels, bears, hyenas)
      - SEALS, SEA LIONS, WALRUSES
      - AARDVARKS
      - HYRAXES AND DASSIES
      - ELEPHANTS
      - SEA COWS (e.g., manatees, dugongs)
      - ODD-TOED HOOFED MAMMALS (e.g., horses, rhinoceroses, tapirs)
      - EVEN-TOED MAMMALS (e.g., hogs, cattle, camels, hippopotamuses)
    - NONPLACENTAL MAMMALS
      - POUCHED MAMMALS (e.g., kangaroos, koalas, oppossums)

Dolphin (bottom) and pilot whale (top)

Dolphin

Killer whale

Humpback whales

NOTEPAD

These marine mammals are divided into two smaller groups by scientists. One group is porpoises and whales with teeth. The other group is whales with baleen. The baleen whales have large, flat, irregular surfaces in their mouths instead of teeth.

Examples of porpoises and whales with teeth: sperm whales, narwhals, beluga whales, porpoises, dolphins, and killer whales.

Examples of baleen whales: gray whales, right whales, fin-backed whales, and humpback whales.

11

Bats

Scientific Name: *Order Chiroptera*
How to Say It: KEH•ROP•TER•AH

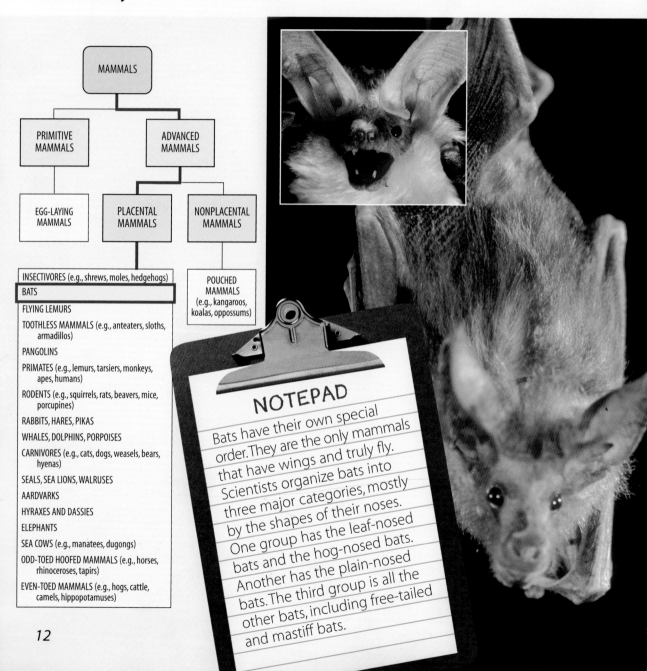

MAMMALS

PRIMITIVE MAMMALS

ADVANCED MAMMALS

EGG-LAYING MAMMALS

PLACENTAL MAMMALS

NONPLACENTAL MAMMALS

INSECTIVORES (e.g., shrews, moles, hedgehogs)

BATS

FLYING LEMURS

TOOTHLESS MAMMALS (e.g., anteaters, sloths, armadillos)

PANGOLINS

PRIMATES (e.g., lemurs, tarsiers, monkeys, apes, humans)

RODENTS (e.g., squirrels, rats, beavers, mice, porcupines)

RABBITS, HARES, PIKAS

WHALES, DOLPHINS, PORPOISES

CARNIVORES (e.g., cats, dogs, weasels, bears, hyenas)

SEALS, SEA LIONS, WALRUSES

AARDVARKS

HYRAXES AND DASSIES

ELEPHANTS

SEA COWS (e.g., manatees, dugongs)

ODD-TOED HOOFED MAMMALS (e.g., horses, rhinoceroses, tapirs)

EVEN-TOED MAMMALS (e.g., hogs, cattle, camels, hippopotamuses)

POUCHED MAMMALS (e.g., kangaroos, koalas, oppossums)

NOTEPAD

Bats have their own special order. They are the only mammals that have wings and truly fly. Scientists organize bats into three major categories, mostly by the shapes of their noses. One group has the leaf-nosed bats and the hog-nosed bats. Another has the plain-nosed bats. The third group is all the other bats, including free-tailed and mastiff bats.

"Flying Lemurs"

Scientific Name: *Order Dermoptera*
How to Say It: DER•MOP•TER•AH

NOTEPAD

The furry mammals in this order don't really fly. And they're not really lemurs (which are primates). But they do climb, jump, and glide through the high treetops of Asia. They glide using a special wing-like membrane between their front and back limbs.

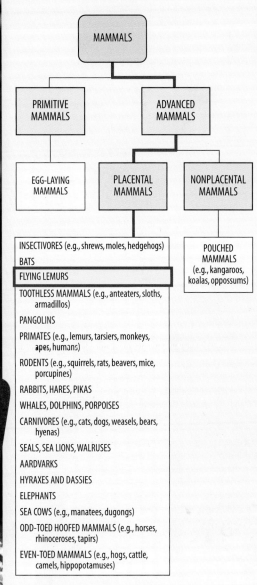

MAMMALS

- PRIMITIVE MAMMALS
- ADVANCED MAMMALS

PRIMITIVE MAMMALS:
- EGG-LAYING MAMMALS

ADVANCED MAMMALS:
- PLACENTAL MAMMALS
- NONPLACENTAL MAMMALS

PLACENTAL MAMMALS:
INSECTIVORES (e.g., shrews, moles, hedgehogs)
BATS
FLYING LEMURS
TOOTHLESS MAMMALS (e.g., anteaters, sloths, armadillos)
PANGOLINS
PRIMATES (e.g., lemurs, tarsiers, monkeys, apes, humans)
RODENTS (e.g., squirrels, rats, beavers, mice, porcupines)
RABBITS, HARES, PIKAS
WHALES, DOLPHINS, PORPOISES
CARNIVORES (e.g., cats, dogs, weasels, bears, hyenas)
SEALS, SEA LIONS, WALRUSES
AARDVARKS
HYRAXES AND DASSIES
ELEPHANTS
SEA COWS (e.g., manatees, dugongs)
ODD-TOED HOOFED MAMMALS (e.g., horses, rhinoceroses, tapirs)
EVEN-TOED MAMMALS (e.g., hogs, cattle, camels, hippopotamuses)

NONPLACENTAL MAMMALS:
POUCHED MAMMALS (e.g., kangaroos, koalas, oppossums)

13

Toothless Mammals

Scientific Name: *Order Edentata*
How to Say It: EE•DEN•TAH•TAH

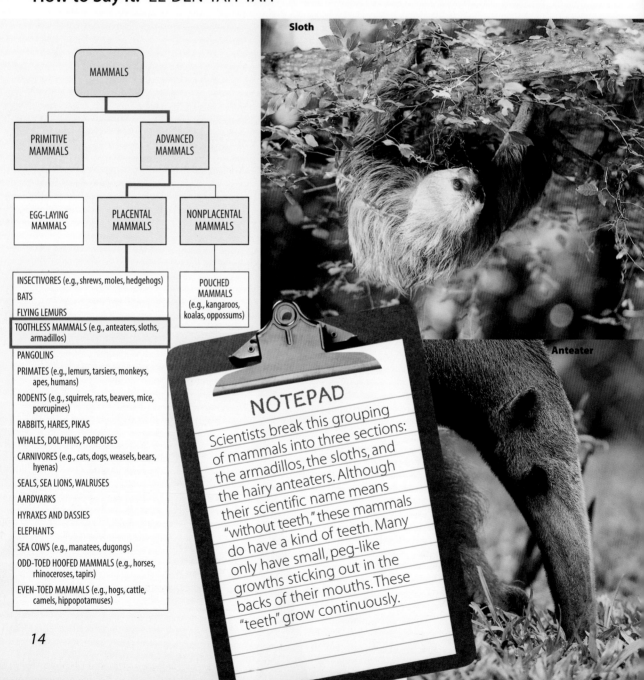

Sloth

Anteater

MAMMALS

PRIMITIVE MAMMALS

ADVANCED MAMMALS

EGG-LAYING MAMMALS

PLACENTAL MAMMALS

NONPLACENTAL MAMMALS

INSECTIVORES (e.g., shrews, moles, hedgehogs)

BATS

FLYING LEMURS

TOOTHLESS MAMMALS (e.g., anteaters, sloths, armadillos)

PANGOLINS

PRIMATES (e.g., lemurs, tarsiers, monkeys, apes, humans)

RODENTS (e.g., squirrels, rats, beavers, mice, porcupines)

RABBITS, HARES, PIKAS

WHALES, DOLPHINS, PORPOISES

CARNIVORES (e.g., cats, dogs, weasels, bears, hyenas)

SEALS, SEA LIONS, WALRUSES

AARDVARKS

HYRAXES AND DASSIES

ELEPHANTS

SEA COWS (e.g., manatees, dugongs)

ODD-TOED HOOFED MAMMALS (e.g., horses, rhinoceroses, tapirs)

EVEN-TOED MAMMALS (e.g., hogs, cattle, camels, hippopotamuses)

POUCHED MAMMALS (e.g., kangaroos, koalas, oppossums)

NOTEPAD

Scientists break this grouping of mammals into three sections: the armadillos, the sloths, and the hairy anteaters. Although their scientific name means "without teeth," these mammals do have a kind of teeth. Many only have small, peg-like growths sticking out in the backs of their mouths. These "teeth" grow continuously.

14

Hyraxes and Dassies

Scientific Name: *Order Hyracoidae*
How to Say It: HI•RAH•COY•DAY

Hyrax

NOTEPAD

These small, rabbit-sized mammals are found mostly in Africa. Scientists believe there are 12 species, or kinds of hyraxes. They group the species into three main categories: the rock hyraxes, the bush hyraxes, and the tree hyraxes.

MAMMALS

PRIMITIVE MAMMALS

ADVANCED MAMMALS

EGG-LAYING MAMMALS

PLACENTAL MAMMALS

NONPLACENTAL MAMMALS

INSECTIVORES (e.g., shrews, moles, hedgehogs)

BATS

FLYING LEMURS

TOOTHLESS MAMMALS (e.g., anteaters, sloths, armadillos)

PANGOLINS

PRIMATES (e.g., lemurs, tarsiers, monkeys, apes, humans)

RODENTS (e.g., squirrels, rats, beavers, mice, porcupines)

RABBITS, HARES, PIKAS

WHALES, DOLPHINS, PORPOISES

CARNIVORES (e.g., cats, dogs, weasels, bears, hyenas)

SEALS, SEA LIONS, WALRUSES

AARDVARKS

HYRAXES AND DASSIES

ELEPHANTS

SEA COWS (e.g., manatees, dugongs)

ODD-TOED HOOFED MAMMALS (e.g., horses, rhinoceroses, tapirs)

EVEN-TOED MAMMALS (e.g., hogs, cattle, camels, hippopotamuses)

POUCHED MAMMALS (e.g., kangaroos, koalas, oppossums)

Insect-Eating Mammals (Insectivores)

Scientific Name: *Order Insectivora*
How to Say It: IN·SEK·TIH·VOR·AH

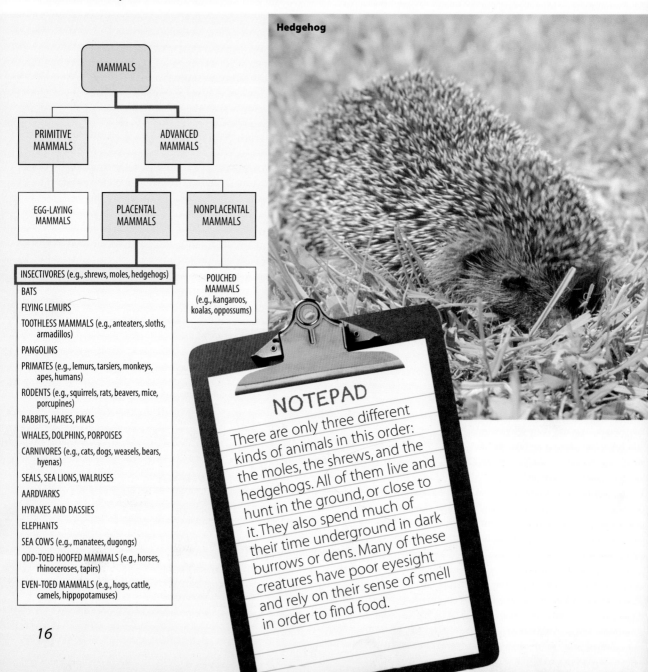

Hedgehog

MAMMALS

PRIMITIVE MAMMALS

ADVANCED MAMMALS

EGG-LAYING MAMMALS

PLACENTAL MAMMALS

NONPLACENTAL MAMMALS

INSECTIVORES (e.g., shrews, moles, hedgehogs)

POUCHED MAMMALS (e.g., kangaroos, koalas, opossums)

BATS

FLYING LEMURS

TOOTHLESS MAMMALS (e.g., anteaters, sloths, armadillos)

PANGOLINS

PRIMATES (e.g., lemurs, tarsiers, monkeys, apes, humans)

RODENTS (e.g., squirrels, rats, beavers, mice, porcupines)

RABBITS, HARES, PIKAS

WHALES, DOLPHINS, PORPOISES

CARNIVORES (e.g., cats, dogs, weasels, bears, hyenas)

SEALS, SEA LIONS, WALRUSES

AARDVARKS

HYRAXES AND DASSIES

ELEPHANTS

SEA COWS (e.g., manatees, dugongs)

ODD-TOED HOOFED MAMMALS (e.g., horses, rhinoceroses, tapirs)

EVEN-TOED MAMMALS (e.g., hogs, cattle, camels, hippopotamuses)

NOTEPAD

There are only three different kinds of animals in this order: the moles, the shrews, and the hedgehogs. All of them live and hunt in the ground, or close to it. They also spend much of their time underground in dark burrows or dens. Many of these creatures have poor eyesight and rely on their sense of smell in order to find food.

Egg-Laying Mammals

Scientific Name: *Order Monotremata*
How to Say It: MAH·NO·TREE·MAH·TAH

Spiny anteater (echidna)

NOTEPAD

These are some of the most ancient kinds of mammals. There are only two groups of these creatures: the spiny anteaters (also called echidnas) and the platypuses. Even though these animals are mammals, they lay eggs! In fact, they are the only egg-laying mammals on Earth!

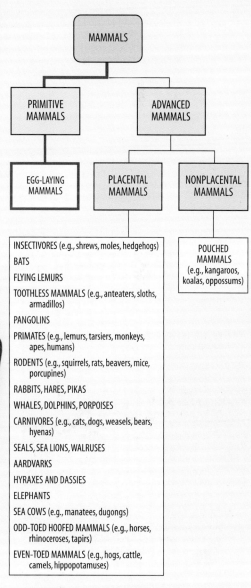

MAMMALS
- PRIMITIVE MAMMALS
  - EGG-LAYING MAMMALS
- ADVANCED MAMMALS
  - PLACENTAL MAMMALS
    - INSECTIVORES (e.g., shrews, moles, hedgehogs)
    - BATS
    - FLYING LEMURS
    - TOOTHLESS MAMMALS (e.g., anteaters, sloths, armadillos)
    - PANGOLINS
    - PRIMATES (e.g., lemurs, tarsiers, monkeys, apes, humans)
    - RODENTS (e.g., squirrels, rats, beavers, mice, porcupines)
    - RABBITS, HARES, PIKAS
    - WHALES, DOLPHINS, PORPOISES
    - CARNIVORES (e.g., cats, dogs, weasels, bears, hyenas)
    - SEALS, SEA LIONS, WALRUSES
    - AARDVARKS
    - HYRAXES AND DASSIES
    - ELEPHANTS
    - SEA COWS (e.g., manatees, dugongs)
    - ODD-TOED HOOFED MAMMALS (e.g., horses, rhinoceroses, tapirs)
    - EVEN-TOED MAMMALS (e.g., hogs, cattle, camels, hippopotamuses)
  - NONPLACENTAL MAMMALS
    - POUCHED MAMMALS (e.g., kangaroos, koalas, oppossums)

Rabbits, Hares, and Pikas

Scientific Name: *Order Lagomorpha*

How to Say It: LA•GO•MORE•FAH

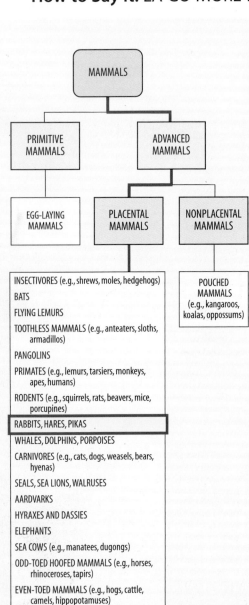

- MAMMALS
  - PRIMITIVE MAMMALS
    - EGG-LAYING MAMMALS
  - ADVANCED MAMMALS
    - PLACENTAL MAMMALS
      - INSECTIVORES (e.g., shrews, moles, hedgehogs)
      - BATS
      - FLYING LEMURS
      - TOOTHLESS MAMMALS (e.g., anteaters, sloths, armadillos)
      - PANGOLINS
      - PRIMATES (e.g., lemurs, tarsiers, monkeys, apes, humans)
      - RODENTS (e.g., squirrels, rats, beavers, mice, porcupines)
      - RABBITS, HARES, PIKAS
      - WHALES, DOLPHINS, PORPOISES
      - CARNIVORES (e.g., cats, dogs, weasels, bears, hyenas)
      - SEALS, SEA LIONS, WALRUSES
      - AARDVARKS
      - HYRAXES AND DASSIES
      - ELEPHANTS
      - SEA COWS (e.g., manatees, dugongs)
      - ODD-TOED HOOFED MAMMALS (e.g., horses, rhinoceroses, tapirs)
      - EVEN-TOED MAMMALS (e.g., hogs, cattle, camels, hippopotamuses)
    - NONPLACENTAL MAMMALS
      - POUCHED MAMMALS (e.g., kangaroos, koalas, oppossums)

Cottontail rabbit

Rabbit

Snowshoe hare

Pika

NOTEPAD

These creatures are commonly divided into two major groups: the rabbits and hares, and the pikas. All of these kinds of animals are furry creatures that feed mostly on plants. A special feature of this kind of mammal is two sets of front teeth, one behind the other.

Noteworthy: What's the difference between a rabbit and a hare? Rabbit babies are born hairless, blind, and helpless. Hare newborns are born furred, with eyes open, and are able to hop within minutes after birth.

Pouched Mammals (Marsupials)

Scientific Name: *Order Marsupia*
How to Say It: MAR•SOO•PEE•YA

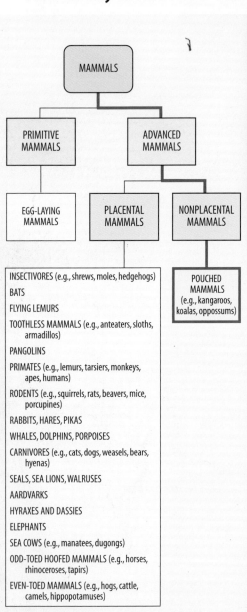

MAMMALS
- PRIMITIVE MAMMALS
  - EGG-LAYING MAMMALS
- ADVANCED MAMMALS
  - PLACENTAL MAMMALS
    - INSECTIVORES (e.g., shrews, moles, hedgehogs)
    - BATS
    - FLYING LEMURS
    - TOOTHLESS MAMMALS (e.g., anteaters, sloths, armadillos)
    - PANGOLINS
    - PRIMATES (e.g., lemurs, tarsiers, monkeys, apes, humans)
    - RODENTS (e.g., squirrels, rats, beavers, mice, porcupines)
    - RABBITS, HARES, PIKAS
    - WHALES, DOLPHINS, PORPOISES
    - CARNIVORES (e.g., cats, dogs, weasels, bears, hyenas)
    - SEALS, SEA LIONS, WALRUSES
    - AARDVARKS
    - HYRAXES AND DASSIES
    - ELEPHANTS
    - SEA COWS (e.g., manatees, dugongs)
    - ODD-TOED HOOFED MAMMALS (e.g., horses, rhinoceroses, tapirs)
    - EVEN-TOED MAMMALS (e.g., hogs, cattle, camels, hippopotamuses)
  - NONPLACENTAL MAMMALS
    - POUCHED MAMMALS (e.g., kangaroos, koalas, oppossums)

Wallaby

Kangaroo

Koala

Wombat

NOTEPAD

Most females of this order have pouches on the outside of their bellies. The pouches are home to newborns that emerge from their mothers before they are fully mature. The newborns crawl into the pouches and stay there for weeks or months. They develop inside, where it is warm and soft. When they are fully developed, they crawl out of the pouches and into the world.

Noteworthy: Not all marsupials have pouches from birth. Some females develop them when they are ready to have young.

Gnawing Mammals (Rodents)

Scientific Name: *Order Rodentia*
How to Say It: RO•DEN•SHAH

MAMMALS

PRIMITIVE MAMMALS

ADVANCED MAMMALS

EGG-LAYING MAMMALS

PLACENTAL MAMMALS

NONPLACENTAL MAMMALS

INSECTIVORES (e.g., shrews, moles, hedgehogs)

BATS

FLYING LEMURS

TOOTHLESS MAMMALS (e.g., anteaters, sloths, armadillos)

PANGOLINS

PRIMATES (e.g., lemurs, tarsiers, monkeys, apes, humans)

RODENTS (e.g., squirrels, rats, beavers, mice, porcupines)

RABBITS, HARES, PIKAS

WHALES, DOLPHINS, PORPOISES

CARNIVORES (e.g., cats, dogs, weasels, bears, hyenas)

SEALS, SEA LIONS, WALRUSES

AARDVARKS

HYRAXES AND DASSIES

ELEPHANTS

SEA COWS (e.g., manatees, dugongs)

ODD-TOED HOOFED MAMMALS (e.g., horses, rhinoceroses, tapirs)

EVEN-TOED MAMMALS (e.g., hogs, cattle, camels, hippopotamuses)

POUCHED MAMMALS (e.g., kangaroos, koalas, oppossums)

Beaver

Ground squirrels

Marmot

Muskrat

Rat

NOTEPAD

There are more of these kinds of mammals than any other kind. Most rodents are ground-dwelling animals with short hair. They also have teeth that they use for gnawing and biting. As a rodent's teeth get worn down, they grow back. Mammals in this group include beavers, chipmunks, squirrels, marmots, mice, rats, lemmings, muskrats, hamsters, gerbils, gophers, and jerboas.

Seals, Sea Lions, and Walruses

Scientific Name: *Order Pinnipedia*
How to Say It: PIN•NEH•PEE•DEE•UH

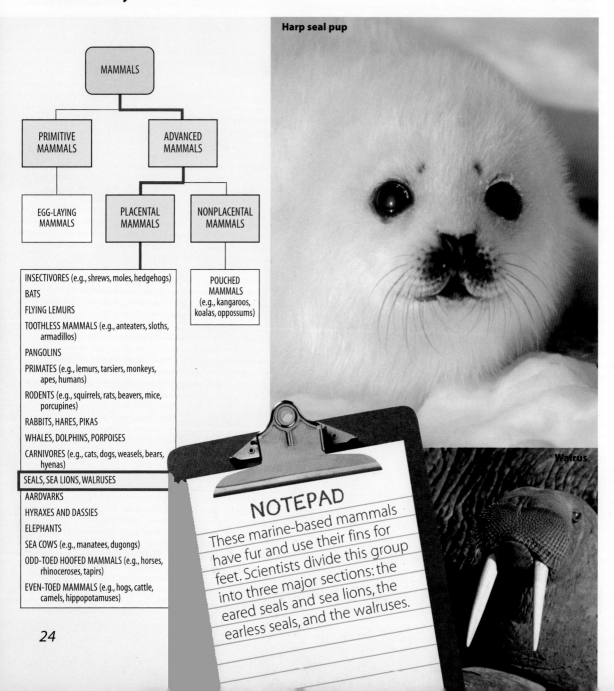

Harp seal pup

Walrus

Classification Chart

- MAMMALS
  - PRIMITIVE MAMMALS
    - EGG-LAYING MAMMALS
  - ADVANCED MAMMALS
    - PLACENTAL MAMMALS
      - INSECTIVORES (e.g., shrews, moles, hedgehogs)
      - BATS
      - FLYING LEMURS
      - TOOTHLESS MAMMALS (e.g., anteaters, sloths, armadillos)
      - PANGOLINS
      - PRIMATES (e.g., lemurs, tarsiers, monkeys, apes, humans)
      - RODENTS (e.g., squirrels, rats, beavers, mice, porcupines)
      - RABBITS, HARES, PIKAS
      - WHALES, DOLPHINS, PORPOISES
      - CARNIVORES (e.g., cats, dogs, weasels, bears, hyenas)
      - SEALS, SEA LIONS, WALRUSES
      - AARDVARKS
      - HYRAXES AND DASSIES
      - ELEPHANTS
      - SEA COWS (e.g., manatees, dugongs)
      - ODD-TOED HOOFED MAMMALS (e.g., horses, rhinoceroses, tapirs)
      - EVEN-TOED MAMMALS (e.g., hogs, cattle, camels, hippopotamuses)
    - NONPLACENTAL MAMMALS
      - POUCHED MAMMALS (e.g., kangaroos, koalas, oppossums)

NOTEPAD

These marine-based mammals have fur and use their fins for feet. Scientists divide this group into three major sections: the eared seals and sea lions, the earless seals, and the walruses.

24

Manatees and Dugongs (Sea Cows)

Scientific Name: *Order Sirenia*
How to Say It: SE•RE•NEE•YA

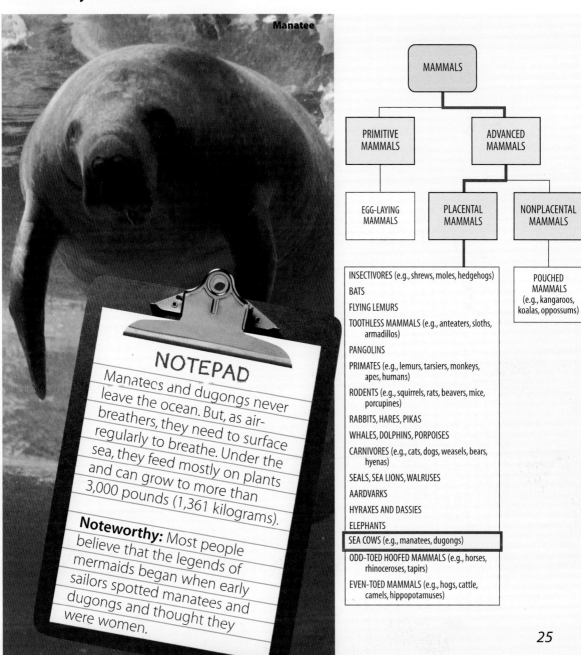

Manatee

MAMMALS

PRIMITIVE MAMMALS

ADVANCED MAMMALS

EGG-LAYING MAMMALS

PLACENTAL MAMMALS

NONPLACENTAL MAMMALS

INSECTIVORES (e.g., shrews, moles, hedgehogs)

BATS

FLYING LEMURS

TOOTHLESS MAMMALS (e.g., anteaters, sloths, armadillos)

PANGOLINS

PRIMATES (e.g., lemurs, tarsiers, monkeys, apes, humans)

RODENTS (e.g., squirrels, rats, beavers, mice, porcupines)

RABBITS, HARES, PIKAS

WHALES, DOLPHINS, PORPOISES

CARNIVORES (e.g., cats, dogs, weasels, bears, hyenas)

SEALS, SEA LIONS, WALRUSES

AARDVARKS

HYRAXES AND DASSIES

ELEPHANTS

SEA COWS (e.g., manatees, dugongs)

ODD-TOED HOOFED MAMMALS (e.g., horses, rhinoceroses, tapirs)

EVEN-TOED MAMMALS (e.g., hogs, cattle, camels, hippopotamuses)

POUCHED MAMMALS (e.g., kangaroos, koalas, oppossums)

NOTEPAD

Manatees and dugongs never leave the ocean. But, as air-breathers, they need to surface regularly to breathe. Under the sea, they feed mostly on plants and can grow to more than 3,000 pounds (1,361 kilograms).

Noteworthy: Most people believe that the legends of mermaids began when early sailors spotted manatees and dugongs and thought they were women.

Primates

Scientific Name: *Order Primates*
How to Say It: PRY•MAYTS

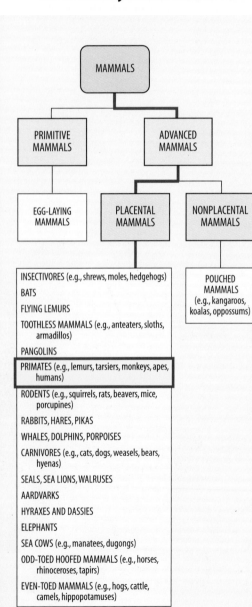

- MAMMALS
  - PRIMITIVE MAMMALS
    - EGG-LAYING MAMMALS
  - ADVANCED MAMMALS
    - PLACENTAL MAMMALS
      - INSECTIVORES (e.g., shrews, moles, hedgehogs)
      - BATS
      - FLYING LEMURS
      - TOOTHLESS MAMMALS (e.g., anteaters, sloths, armadillos)
      - PANGOLINS
      - PRIMATES (e.g., lemurs, tarsiers, monkeys, apes, humans)
      - RODENTS (e.g., squirrels, rats, beavers, mice, porcupines)
      - RABBITS, HARES, PIKAS
      - WHALES, DOLPHINS, PORPOISES
      - CARNIVORES (e.g., cats, dogs, weasels, bears, hyenas)
      - SEALS, SEA LIONS, WALRUSES
      - AARDVARKS
      - HYRAXES AND DASSIES
      - ELEPHANTS
      - SEA COWS (e.g., manatees, dugongs)
      - ODD-TOED HOOFED MAMMALS (e.g., horses, rhinoceroses, tapirs)
      - EVEN-TOED MAMMALS (e.g., hogs, cattle, camels, hippopotamuses)
    - NONPLACENTAL MAMMALS
      - POUCHED MAMMALS (e.g., kangaroos, koalas, oppossums)

Lemur

Humans

Orangutan

Loris

Chimpanzee

NOTEPAD

This is the order to which humans belong. Most scientists organize the primates into two major groupings, according to the kind of nose each animal has. One group is the longer-snouted mammals. The other group is the shorter-snouted mammals.

Examples of longer-snouted mammals: tree shrews, lemurs, aye-ayes, lorises, pottos, and tarsiers.

Examples of shorter-snouted mammals: marmosets, baboons, monkeys, gibbons, gorillas, chimpanzees, orangutans, and humans.

Elephants

Scientific Name: *Order Proboscidea*
How to Say It: PRO•BOS•SID•DI•AH

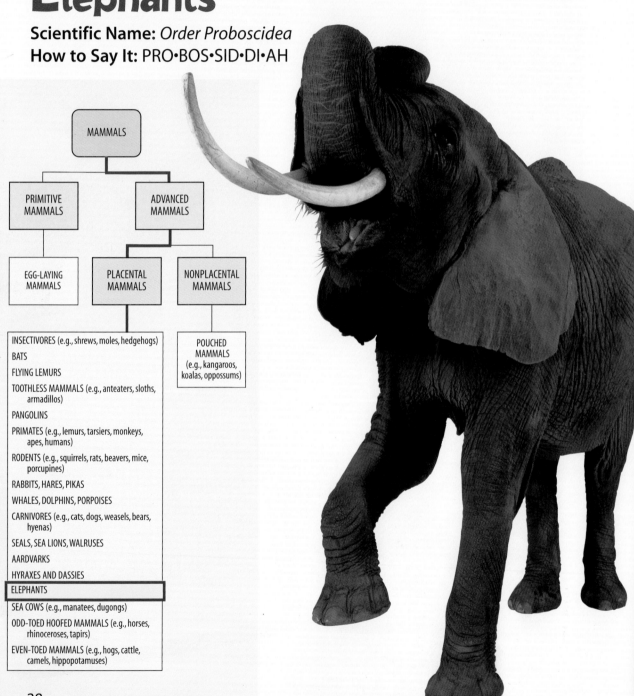

```
                    ┌──────────┐
                    │ MAMMALS  │
                    └────┬─────┘
            ┌────────────┴────────────┐
      ┌───────────┐            ┌───────────┐
      │ PRIMITIVE │            │ ADVANCED  │
      │ MAMMALS   │            │ MAMMALS   │
      └─────┬─────┘            └─────┬─────┘
            │              ┌─────────┴─────────┐
     ┌────────────┐  ┌────────────┐  ┌──────────────┐
     │ EGG-LAYING │  │ PLACENTAL  │  │ NONPLACENTAL │
     │ MAMMALS    │  │ MAMMALS    │  │ MAMMALS      │
     └────────────┘  └─────┬──────┘  └──────┬───────┘
```

INSECTIVORES (e.g., shrews, moles, hedgehogs)

BATS

FLYING LEMURS

TOOTHLESS MAMMALS (e.g., anteaters, sloths, armadillos)

PANGOLINS

PRIMATES (e.g., lemurs, tarsiers, monkeys, apes, humans)

RODENTS (e.g., squirrels, rats, beavers, mice, porcupines)

RABBITS, HARES, PIKAS

WHALES, DOLPHINS, PORPOISES

CARNIVORES (e.g., cats, dogs, weasels, bears, hyenas)

SEALS, SEA LIONS, WALRUSES

AARDVARKS

HYRAXES AND DASSIES

ELEPHANTS

SEA COWS (e.g., manatees, dugongs)

ODD-TOED HOOFED MAMMALS (e.g., horses, rhinoceroses, tapirs)

EVEN-TOED MAMMALS (e.g., hogs, cattle, camels, hippopotamuses)

POUCHED MAMMALS (e.g., kangaroos, koalas, oppossums)

NOTEPAD

Elephants are huge animals that make up a mammal order all on their own. Their scientific name comes from the word *proboscis*, which means nose, snout, or trunk. They are the largest and heaviest of all land mammals. They are also some of the longest lived.

Noteworthy: An elephant can eat up to 500 pounds (227 kilograms) of food each day, and can drink up to 40 gallons (151 liters) of water at once!

Pangolins

Scientific Name: *Order Pholidata*

How to Say It: FO•LI•DAH•TAH

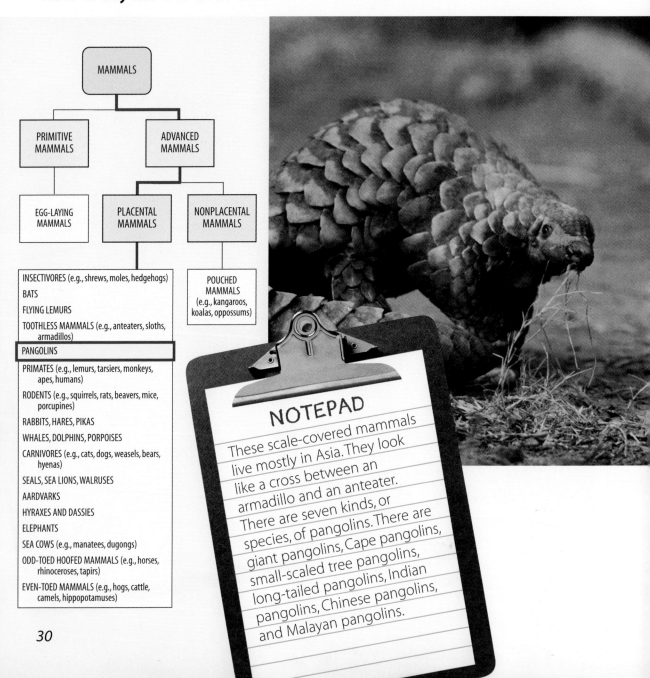

```
                    ┌──────────────┐
                    │   MAMMALS    │
                    └──────┬───────┘
            ┌──────────────┴──────────────┐
      ┌───────────┐              ┌──────────────┐
      │ PRIMITIVE │              │   ADVANCED   │
      │  MAMMALS  │              │   MAMMALS    │
      └─────┬─────┘              └──────┬───────┘
            │              ┌────────────┴────────────┐
      ┌───────────┐  ┌───────────┐          ┌──────────────┐
      │ EGG-LAYING│  │ PLACENTAL │          │ NONPLACENTAL │
      │  MAMMALS  │  │  MAMMALS  │          │   MAMMALS    │
      └───────────┘  └─────┬─────┘          └──────┬───────┘
```

INSECTIVORES (e.g., shrews, moles, hedgehogs)

BATS

FLYING LEMURS

TOOTHLESS MAMMALS (e.g., anteaters, sloths, armadillos)

PANGOLINS

PRIMATES (e.g., lemurs, tarsiers, monkeys, apes, humans)

RODENTS (e.g., squirrels, rats, beavers, mice, porcupines)

RABBITS, HARES, PIKAS

WHALES, DOLPHINS, PORPOISES

CARNIVORES (e.g., cats, dogs, weasels, bears, hyenas)

SEALS, SEA LIONS, WALRUSES

AARDVARKS

HYRAXES AND DASSIES

ELEPHANTS

SEA COWS (e.g., manatees, dugongs)

ODD-TOED HOOFED MAMMALS (e.g., horses, rhinoceroses, tapirs)

EVEN-TOED MAMMALS (e.g., hogs, cattle, camels, hippopotamuses)

POUCHED MAMMALS (e.g., kangaroos, koalas, oppossums)

NOTEPAD

These scale-covered mammals live mostly in Asia. They look like a cross between an armadillo and an anteater. There are seven kinds, or species, of pangolins. There are giant pangolins, Cape pangolins, small-scaled tree pangolins, long-tailed pangolins, Indian pangolins, Chinese pangolins, and Malayan pangolins.

Aardvarks

Scientific Name: *Order Tubulidentata*
How to Say It: TOO•BEW•LE•DEN•TAH•TAH

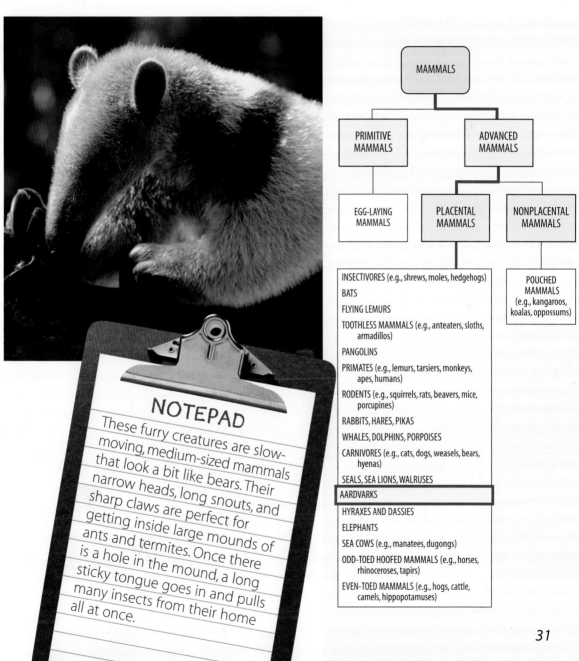

```
                    ┌─────────────┐
                    │   MAMMALS   │
                    └─────────────┘
              ┌───────────┴───────────┐
       ┌──────────────┐      ┌──────────────┐
       │  PRIMITIVE   │      │   ADVANCED   │
       │   MAMMALS    │      │   MAMMALS    │
       └──────────────┘      └──────────────┘
              │           ┌───────┴────────┐
       ┌──────────────┐ ┌──────────┐ ┌──────────────┐
       │  EGG-LAYING  │ │PLACENTAL │ │ NONPLACENTAL │
       │   MAMMALS    │ │ MAMMALS  │ │   MAMMALS    │
       └──────────────┘ └──────────┘ └──────────────┘
```

INSECTIVORES (e.g., shrews, moles, hedgehogs)

BATS

FLYING LEMURS

TOOTHLESS MAMMALS (e.g., anteaters, sloths, armadillos)

PANGOLINS

PRIMATES (e.g., lemurs, tarsiers, monkeys, apes, humans)

RODENTS (e.g., squirrels, rats, beavers, mice, porcupines)

RABBITS, HARES, PIKAS

WHALES, DOLPHINS, PORPOISES

CARNIVORES (e.g., cats, dogs, weasels, bears, hyenas)

SEALS, SEA LIONS, WALRUSES

AARDVARKS

HYRAXES AND DASSIES

ELEPHANTS

SEA COWS (e.g., manatees, dugongs)

ODD-TOED HOOFED MAMMALS (e.g., horses, rhinoceroses, tapirs)

EVEN-TOED MAMMALS (e.g., hogs, cattle, camels, hippopotamuses)

POUCHED MAMMALS (e.g., kangaroos, koalas, oppossums)

NOTEPAD

These furry creatures are slow-moving, medium-sized mammals that look a bit like bears. Their narrow heads, long snouts, and sharp claws are perfect for getting inside large mounds of ants and termites. Once there is a hole in the mound, a long sticky tongue goes in and pulls many insects from their home all at once.

Glossary

Carnivore an animal that eats mainly meat.

Cud food that has not been digested that some animals bring up from their stomachs to chew again.

Herbivore an animal that eats mainly grass.

Mammal any animal that has a backbone, feeds its newborn milk from the mother's body, and is relatively covered with hair.

Marsupial a large group of animals in which the female carries her young in a pouch on her abdomen.

Membrane a very thin layer of tissue or skin that covers certain organs or cells.

Placental mammal a mammal that develops in its mother's womb and receives nutritious substances from the yolk-like placenta that nourishes it before birth.

Primate any member of the group of intelligent mammals, including humans.

For More Information

Books

Harman, Amanda. *Manatees & Dugongs (*Endangered*).* Tarrytown, NY: Benchmark Books, 1997.

Jeunesse, Gallimard. *Mammals: Whales, Panthers, Rats, and Bats: The Characteristics of Mammals from Around the World* (Voyages of Discovery)**.** New York, NY: Scholastic Trade, 1997.

Ricciuti, Edward. *What On Earth Is a Pangolin?* (What On Earth). Woodbridge, CT: Blackbirch Press, 1994.

Tesar, Jenny. *What On Earth Is an Echidna?* (What On Earth). Woodbridge, CT: Blackbirch Press, 1995.

Web Sites

Cetacea

A great resource page for dolphin, whale, and porpoise information— www.geocities.com/RainForest/canopy/1599

Marsupial Mammals

Facts and photographs about marsupials and their habitat—www.ucmp.berkeley.edu/mammal/ marsupial/marsupial.html

Index